IN BEAUTY WE ARE MADE VISIBLE

In Beauty We Are Made Visible
© Christine Morro, 2022.

Books may be purchased in quantity and/or special sales by contacting the publisher. All such inquiries related to bulk order matters should be addressed to:

Middle Creek Publishing & Audio
9167 Pueblo Mountain Park Road
Beulah, CO 81023

editor@middlecreekpublishing.com
(719) 369-9050

First Paperback Edition, 2022
ISBN: 978-1-957483-01-6

Cover Image & Design: Christine Morro
Author Image: Victor Puccio

Printed in the United States

IN BEAUTY WE ARE MADE VISIBLE

Thank you for honoring beauty

Christine Morro

Middle Creek Publishing
Beulah, CO   USA
↑

"The beauty of things was born before eyes and sufficient to itself, the heart-breaking beauty will remain when there is no heart to break for it"

Robinson Jeffers

For my mother and the memory of my dear father

thank you for your patience and love

OUR SKIN IS OF EARTH

Rivered glyphs of schist, the utterances of sediment
leaves of poplar whispering to the balsamic moon
Awake to life coursing in the fissured bark
of a four hundred-year old chestnut tree
Earth literacy begins with contact
Press your palm to the heart of Earth
primary language is born from receptivity
Prayers carried on the tongues of acequias
incantations rising from water and stone
Tracing contours of mountains
an ancient contract of belonging
Our skin is of earth

WHEN ROOF WAS MADE OF SKY

We honored and celebrated
earth's exhale into the seam of dawn
Passing through gates of rime
we connected to the land through
ancestral currents held in water's memory
Ritual and ceremony courting
wolf, bear, silver horn of the moon
as stars drift down fingers tipped with fire
Once, long ago we were all imagined
by earth   winged and rhizomic
reading moss on stone as scripture
Our language governed by the rhythm
of seasons by sun and moon
our songs became our maps
We walked lightly within our stories
drinking from the river

wyrd: (old English)
fate, destiny; becoming

A towering stone of gneiss
blooms of lichen the color of
mist and wind, *terre vert*
plumes curl like breath
sending signals skyward
Enter this province of mystery
A prayer to emptiness
the inner light of absence
Dark lunate a place that asks
us to embody wilderness
Drop the map and allow an
ancient sacred trust
Shelter in life unfolding

EVENTIDE

At the edge of night the world becomes more visible to our ears
to the feeling part of our being we see with the hearing eye

Light combs the surface of pond

reed grass   sedge

soft floor of earth

mind meets feet where

end descends into beginning

Receptive terrain of our skin

modulates relations of trust

breath travels its sacred channel

currency of bone and spirit

Touch and be touched

earth's deepest caverns

sediment speaks secrets

mineral   stone   alluvial silt

crepuscular voices

slip like water over rock

Listen to the sound spell
follow the lunar umbilicus
nature discloses herself as magic
the heart our primary observer
Speech of stones carry truths
to story us into the underland
Let earth change you, heal you back
and suddenly in the violet dark

Stubborn red berries adorn

a monochrome landscape

Washed in umbered tones

faint crescent of light held by sky

like breath on this cold morning

Stand near the edge of Sagg Pond

on a winters day ocean enters

a grip on the ear of the heart

Into the present we are drawn

Move small into these new depths

An invitation waking inside of dawn

To weave ourselves back into relationship with Earth

Listen to what stirs the waters of the body

Let the speech of elemental earth

be where our attention is drawn

For ages and ages we have received instruction

Become intimate with all dimensions of the

ground beneath your feet, attend with devotion to

trees, her roots, urgent mycorrhizal strivings

Keep close company with the sun and moon

the flow of rivers, the tides

Allow your heart to break for the perishable

nature of life

Live in sacred trust with this fracture

Sea algae, wing kelp, tangles of

microcellular Gracilaria

symbiotic tidal rafts of life

the many names for creation

I call acts of devotion

Early morning a serpentine of wrack

A glistening line of marine matter

draws me down to my knees

untangling delicate threads

Mingling with prayers of forest kelp

ruffles of *codium fragile*

To live deliberately into a question

To be taken with awe storied by

the collapse of mystery into language

To descend into intimacy

beyond reason to the sea

Call in the intelligence of soil
tunnel the darkness, endure the stones

Root. Humus. Soul
follow the filaments
the lacy concealed networks

Receive the scriptures of loam
the soles of our feet are this reception

Heed the beckoning voice of the
mycelial underworld

Toes push through ancient layers
of myth anima buckles toward the
edge of the concealed

How can we touch earth more deeply

Enter the nourishing darkness of new moon

Sky plies the glossy threads

of waning moon

the exhale a curl of sea foam

Across the shallows of Sagg Pond

waters of the Atlantic

spill into her restless body

A mingling of elemental wisdom

Sky in awe of what great love

on earth can do

Canis Lupus howls a song of stars

mirroring sky back on itself

Measure of mystery inside

A dream born from fur and presence

Oak and sweet gum

sassafras, river birch and pine

All the vernal world

in her primeval shimmer

Altar cloaked in velvety moss

granite, feldspar, quartz and mica

The sun sharp glint reveals

furrowed lines etched

Place where Catawba flows

Thousands of years

green tongue of spring

Traveler crosses limits

My feet in two worlds

SHELTER (v)

Daily I walk the path along the bluff

then down to Sconset Beach

A practice that teaches me to listen, to attend

Today air stiff with cold

Dried eelgrass, kelp, dark matted feathers of seabirds

Strands of filamentous threads,

cobalt blue fishing net, red Solo cups

The almost unnoticed wonders

entangled along the tideline

To miss any of this world is the taste of despair

POEM AS RELIQUARY

Acknowledging the loss of the lives of

Barbodes tras
Barbodes truncatulus

Cora timucua
Marshallia grandflora

Reciting the names of an additional
sixty-five North American plants,
twenty-two frog species
I say the names of the mite species
who vanished in 2020 almost
slipping by statisticians

I'd like to think of these orchids,
amphibians, conifers as saints
beings of noble lineage
No longer capable of being themselves
Names chanted to remember who
brought us here
Quiet networks of grace

here I learn

water presses light

light pressing mineral, quartz, schist.

a postscript to the main poem, river

warmth seamed by twilight

the trace of a thousand mornings

ochre, copper, meadow-brown

a marbling of silt held in deep time

silence is devotion, dawn a prayer

the flexion of water

currency we name wildness

certainties loosened stones

THE ELSEWHERE OF AFTERNOON RAIN

Incantations of Oleander *oualili*

carried over the Mediterranean

fading blue cords of mountains

From desert

and dreams

to a currents ear

Let the stillness of the night enfold us

Clouds and mountains

Tapering goats' bells

spill like water down the hillside

Tell me how far I am from the outside world

Fern and wild blackberry give themselves

to the river's dream

VESPER | Bone prayer

A fossil star of light governs darkness
bird alight sand-etched ghost wings
a blanket of frost   berry red crown
Walk lightly where the waters are clear
pilgrimage of sun   locus of moon
an initiatory circle   wind-dance
silent loom of dreams
Each weft connects water
to earth to air
woven into a solstice prayer
I seal my vow with breath

owl's soft brown barring

bundles of pine needles
infused with melted snow
golden warmth of flames
vanishing threads of light
a migrating wave
on the verge of elsewhere
Shelter in this emptiness

I FLY OUT OF A HEAVY YEAR LONG CYCLE

Light scant and spare
at the rise of spring's first sun
water speaks, leaning into
This!   Turning the soil of the heart
Tender witness seamed with silence
the first bright song of the red-winged blackbird
a strike of crimson on an ink black wing
Energy plied and woven into a sacred web
currents of water crisscross with close attention
the stillness of the great blue heron undone
her wings unfold the whole of dawn

LUNAR CYCLE | Full Moon

May we wander and lose ourselves
to worn paths of earth
May we live utterly deeply not knowing
May we listen for new stories and await their meanings
May we realize our wounds go beyond the edge of skin
May we love through these fissures and openings
May we fall awake to what calls again and again
May we become sovereign by trusting the great cord
that connects us to mother earth
May we give agency to the charred and trust in
regeneration though we might not see a sign of green
May we never look away
May we pay attention, always

IN WILDNESS WE TRUST

HAUNT

Old Norse, *heimta to lead home*
Shifting light, late afternoon
a finger traces a single line
The invitation across mineral dark
waters wind thrummed surface
Shoaling of iridescent fish
flows out of the present
into where the ancestors dwell
Moonrise, eyes adjust to evenfall
each mellow lap of wave
An initiatory dance

Mist shuttered lake
flower moon blooms
singing a lament to trees
a line of quartz fills
        the fracture
hymns of lichen
repair our wound

Sanskrit *sivyati* "sews," sutra, *sutram* "thread, string;"
Greek" *hymnos* "song;" Latin *suere* "to sew, sew to-
gether;" Old English *siwian* "to stitch, sew, mend,
patch, knit together."

From beyond the fold of hills
and the tides of the sound and bays
reaching over palisades and city contour
Veeries migrate swift on the wing –
through iridescent bands of stars
impatient of the horizon and the
careless ways of the human world
their song remains pure
zorzalito rojizo   wind
on the tongue

EDGE OF THE MOOR

I

Deer emerge the way
the scent of pine releases
from resin between my fingers
Blue fades into softening light
In the inscription of branches
the presence of owl

II

Here where the more solitary
build their nests among cedar and
pitch pine, scrub oak, bayberry and
the infinitely wild lions foot
I want to know the world without
dimming its mystery
Gazing with quiet awe
at blazing star, eastern silvery aster

PARTIAL SOLAR ECLIPSE

as the sky's radiance dims
primrose petals press to form
a yellow lantern on this morning
a prayer mat of silence

how many temples built
bows and salutations made?

Along the curve of moorland
I encounter the place where
turquoise and ultramarine contradict
the thunderous gray of morning
Luskentyre draws voice
to why I am here yet cannot name
words on the tongue
a tenderly bundled offering of sound
passing through as warp and weft
sound flows on breath   *Lios-cinn-tir*
belonging to communication between
intertidal shallows and enduring heath
wind bends coarse dune grass
each blade undulant and fluent
wingspan of the sea

WINGS UNFOLD | Barren field

Altar and offering
slender luminous crescent
finger of Brigit
strikes the first chords of spring
Holy darkness   this limen world
restless as a body of stars
pin prick pulses of light
hold the imprint of the moment
before we were born
Fragile alliance of seed heads
aroused from lassitude
A sharpening love we call sun
Can we name navigational coordinates
courage body the soft ground
Earth's elliptical turn

Each act of witness an ancient ritual

Earth asks us to listen ~

Remembering, we weave the threads of the past to the future

CEREMONY | NEW MOON

I draw a circle of fire
to warm and to receive
that which has not yet been shaped
before thumb presses into clay
fire is the body
breath precedes flesh
in the vastness where earth meets sea
sky and fire kindle life
formless, fire is air
I draw a circle of fire
where listening is the imprint of spiral
Through cycles and seasons
Awaiting that which
has not yet eyes
I draw a circle of fire
flickering embers a skein of geese
smudge of carbon tapers above horizon
I carry the fire

A murmuration of birds
shifting cloud of wings
slips through a sleeve of air
swells into a wave and
disappears like unfinished light

we are this place called love

Snowy owl
follow her silent floating form
as the ear pitching toward
the sound of a temple bell until the last
circular ring disappears

The practice within practice
to be in service to this moment
to endure as the sea endures

with great love

For a long time I stood
not moved beyond earth but
drawn down embedded like a fossil
In the rapture of a Red-tailed Hawk
Fine forest of warm sepia feathers
Pinions stiff with endurance
Kiting through fanning rays
afternoon sun

Broad stretch of salt marsh
extends to the Atlantic

What do we do with these moments that
feel like transmission?
An old Zen master might reply *"nothing"*
Soles of my feet press with great
care for such a world

TWELVE TONES OF BLUE

Shadows of wings as broad as clouds
Blue locates us
The color of skies and of
mystery oceanic and celestial
In the leaves of *indigofera tinctoria*
blue originates in green
Miles Davis plays in this field
of in-between
The light in blue
disappearing from night
into twilight before civic dawn
It is edge it is what comes after edge
Brilliant deeply pigmented hues
rendered from a slurry of bacteria,
water, green-life transmuting
The heat of alchemy a continuous
story of communion and co-creation

In the animist tradition of the
Dogon everything has a soul
a tree, the rain, a stone
A circle of women
their hands clap with the rhythm
of pestle pounding mortar
Awakening indigo from its dreamworld
blue has a soul

REFUGE

how can the heart be only the size of a fist

Mid-winter refuge. Early morning,
the hour we are still invisible
sky in the room
layers thick with cloud
dawn courts the song sparrows

Soft ground of thawing earth
registers their feet
the stillness from which all begins
the yolk from which i tread
secretly into the day

The glow of mountain an inner fire
River carries the scent of neroli
Evening call of Scops Owl
An acoustic destination in the night

Moon travels beyond the ridge
Sulayr   *walking light*
all that we name disappears
Hum of stars, resting between C and C#

RIVER WALK

A crown of stones, goat paths upslope spiny leaves of thistle, an abandoned *cortijo*, roofless and light-filled, no welcome mat, broad canopied chestnut, a different kind of welcome mat prayer draws us down, prayer is wind, it is the deep quiet saturated in sunlight, it is feet to sun-parched earth, it is the secret lives of wild goats whose clacking hooves i hear from across the *barranco*, it is wisdom in the *anahata* chakra of trees, received and transmitted

It is paths recorded by the land, the heart of those who walk them, mapmakers, my feet remember, storied by foot-fall of ancestors, rivered by current, flow braiding water braiding time before mountain and river, invitations of green light, summer's ecstatic dance of poplar, bird song flows with the rush of water, snows from winter, spring rains let the river have its way with you, Mulhacen rises to meet Veleta, guardians of the valley

Strike of yellow on a carbon black wing a small bird with a thick beak, pulls and tugs at flowering purple heads, follow the apse of blue the altar of thistle-eater

Water curls around rock connecting to larger truths, river silt, schist, indivisible keepers the whole history of the mountain

Toothed leaves of chestnut, clusters of green spiny-cups of life revealing millions of years of earth, golden *esparto* and quivering oat grass, the sutras of grasshopper from the monastery on the hilltop mingle with lamenting songs of gypsies, my hands stained red from the ripened fruit of mulberry

Through touch and resonance it is ant who pinches my skin with a sudden sting, it is river flow it is oceanic love beyond fading blue silhouettes of hills, it is holy longing mineralized, it is the sediment laid down quietly and slow, it is warp and weft weaving earth whole by which i do not mean complete, threshed it is the chaff as it takes to the sky and drifts someplace down valley it is wildness rattling the faint of heart, wind reclaiming, wind decolonizing, wind removing husk, bringing us to our knees, carrying dust over mountains from faraway deserts

Let life in as we too must allow death its passage, we can open the gates and praise even the most bewildering, a confluence is an exchange, a sacred meeting in the magic dark of becoming something different

Loosen the jambs, reception is receiving, it is giving ourselves, engaging robustly with a world of elemental attention fall awake to earth's capacity to reciprocate, listen as long as the rivers shall run

Count to twelve buzzing bees, birds tapping charred branches, dogs barking across the valley, life breathes through layers of soil, through the skin of earth, listen for the questions live them fully let go of anything that keeps you moving in meager isolating strides, contemplate the majesty of it all, yes everything four hundred years carrying a lineage of ancestral networks through roots, mycelial conversations, secrets shared across many lives what dies in the heartwood brings new life through ripple, through seed dropped, a story as old as home

THE WEIGHT OF RAIN

on clusters of maple flowers
draws me up
to shift from supine to standing
the exact weight unknown
throughout night the strength of song
in birds' throats accumulates
morning's fluting notes released
through love's narrow channels
the first light of day reveals
a string of pearl clouds
resting in a pillow of
heavy sulfurous clouds
look for roots, origins
through the rough work
our coarse instincts bear
bands of fluorite and quartz
you will not find clarity mining

understand the gods work
while we sleep
as we go about the
dailyness of our lives
the rain, the seasons, the sun
reach beyond the mountain
as light spreads to accord
this strange unfinished
the exact weight unknown

Seals rest in the boundary between matter and the imaginal. On the edge of winter the sea polished by the low sun. I am here in search for the ghost white plumage of Snowy Owl scanning dunes toward the arching cloudless sky. Ruddy ducks buoyant on the surface of the pond, a chevron of geese shifts back and forth into form. In the end it's not what i see that really matters, it's the act of being out on the land like worship, connecting with what is wider, wild. The dialogue between body and the land a reminder of the ancient bond shared with Earth. Glaciers formed this land, depositing silt and gravel. The settling and melting of ice created these ponds. Over the course of thousands of years stones washed over and again in the sea's ancient ritual becoming the sandy spine I stand on.

ARCHIPELAGO IN THE NORTH ATLANTIC
62 00' N 06 47' W

Some landscapes we meet
just once others we have known
through years of return
Intimacy enfolds us outside
the boundary of time
Gesturing invitation
Over Streymoy in the sweep of winds
A living terrain rainwater flows
sluicing over rock and heath
Sparing purple heads of wildflowers
Confirmed movement into sea
basalt cliffs   rough pasture
my boots sink into sodden earth
towers of stones   waymarks
Saints of the earth bear witness
Seabirds wheel a circular wreath
of earth and sky   Clouds detail
A balcony of light
The weight of earth offers her
enduring power   calling us back
pulling us into the deep marrow
the deep green marrow

QUERENCIA

At the easternmost point of Nantucket
The compass rose at Sankaty Lighthouse
reads Spain 3,054 miles

At dawn the wind dies down
I lace up my boots, head out
Sun creates a triangle of light
Earth discloses her magic

Reclaim large areas of peace
our duty is to be such a beacon

We map the earth with our feet
belonging to something more than
ourselves the ritual of walking
connects us to place

Passage reshapes the ground we traverse
Earth remembers us

Mid July I follow the *sendero*
where a fire blazed on the Sierra Nevada.
The remains of centuries old Chestnut
trees stand like charred torsos

I am reminded fire is regeneration
Up through blackened terrain
thistle and blue malva grow
I stand on holy ground

The land a prayer mat, our place
of belonging

How far a circle do we draw to include
the fanning light of the sun as it filters
through tangles of green in the estuary's shallows
the slow plow of Moon Snail
the nacreous luster of the Quahog's inner shell
Oh, stubborn persistence of Marsh Heather
what strange beauty binds these marginal worlds
To be born of Earth's recurrent rhythms
Each breath of our entangled life no less than
Our almost forgotten gods

UNDER GATHERING CLOUDS

The dark sea extends from the horizon
Drawing back into the pull of the tide
Broad brush of water reflects
the late morning sun

The Wampanoag named this land
"The Place of Great Bones"
I kneel beside the arc of a bone
Its size measures several inches beyond my height
Resting my back along the sweep of its contour
My feet extend to the large knobby joint
at the mouth of the Atlantic

I don't know the etymology of Mysticeti
but I sense something primordial
and eternal, an old story
A numinous cord in Gaia's ancient story

I am reminded of the sea inside of us
born of mineral, birth and water
In the silence, through fathoms of darkness
sing and sing your haunting deep song

RITUAL BINDS US

At the opening of mid-winter
pale hues of sky surround pine, cedar
earth a hard crust of frozen snow
hoof prints   a solitary deer met dawn
I glimpse what i was brought here to
The enormous wing a sweeping
cloud dips down to the sea
its soft edges licked by morning sun
This day i mount an altar
a sanctuary to the quiver of loss
to the debris of winter,
in the yolk of waiting
This gift of absence
flying white and silent

Agape, (v) agapao, one of the several Greek words for love.

Early December through March my eyes scan the dunes. The act of bringing a focused gaze tells me somewhere Snowy Owl is here. The Atlantic's elusive winter resident teaches earthliness and confidence to trust that my powers are not separate from the wildness that surrounds me.

Early morning from horizon to shoreline a love letter written with light. This week i honor my father, his passing, the vast presence of devotion. I hold the grief of his absence and give myself to this utterly wild space.

I let each wave impress its continuum rising and falling, unceasingly on the wheel of wind.

Sagaponack, NY

ONCE AGAIN, SPRING

Once again,
for the first time spring
Early morning approaching Sagg Pond
In the exhale of dawn
barely a pale glow
presses into the horizon
Here creation works on itself
I walk lightly without disturbance
heel first, toes spread
White's field, lines and scratches
like an old engraver's plate, not yet
released from night
The imagination wants to reside
in this moment
Voice of Kingfisher heightens the silence
I pause in the urge to respond to his call
and follow the arc of his flight
with the precision of a compass
needle trace the gleam, the flicker of blue
that is his path, the desirable middle
between reeds and the posts of
a weathered mooring

A layer of frost shimmers
Dawn's orange glow   luminous floss
plied with soft easterly wind
dunes clothed in fine Dhaka muslin
Winter's persistent hold

I walk following a circular bed
pine needles soft padding
beneath my boots in these
small hours   seven pine limbs
create a vessel   holding the
not fully lit sky

An ecotone of blue widens
the field between my shoulder blades
The hidden world where
the impress of deer dwells
within the fragrance of pine sap

All that is not held by the intellect belongs
to the deepest aspect of your being

For today I refrain from repeating the given names issued on title or deed of the places I walk. Language arises with the elements, the nuance carried in the wind, the whispers of marsh grass, secrets offered, invitations extended.

The land everywhere speaks. From the tongue rolls currents, susurrations, murmurs. Imbued with spirit. Alive as the Earth herself.

/ \   symbol for prayer, mountain, a bow

I walk treading lightly with the rhythm of my breath ~
without shoes

poetry originates through the soles of our feet

IN BEAUTY WE ARE MADE VISIBLE

Eel grass gleaming sea meadow
storied by the sea herself
the long slow swell of a wave
a reception of white sea foam
water belonging to hollow bones and stars
a spangled boundary of northern gannets
I scribble twelve secret names
and bury all but two in a pocket of sand
bowing, kneeling, unfolding
into the eyes of seal a refuge
embodied presence of ancestors
here where the light empties
Estuaried story of
the merging into new collectives
Draw your hand across the impress
our incompleteness
let the sea contribute toward mystery
Vast body   my body

NORTH HAVEN, NY

February morning, no day to construct with ambition. Mellow bands the color of citrine brighten above the horizon. A slow entrance atop a seat of granite. Quartz dances in the sun's light like water's rippling script.

Twilight teaches us that time is not linear. I am connected to earth through glacial flow in geologic degree under unknown stars in a spiral toward Spring.

The next full moon sees the return of Osprey. Nature's refrain . . .coordinates that keep us bonded in deep trust. Hooked black beaks loaded with cedar twigs, marsh grass, the sea's detritus. Interfold of hours Osprey build their nest.

2.24.20

DEVOTIONAL OFFERING

Resting between copper-hued marsh grass,
in dying stars reborn as delicate chalky shells
kinship lies in a thin membrane called pause
sit here in the undoing
dwell in the living world of tide falling

From breath receding and lifting
a bind of shorebirds alights
leggy sandpipers settle on a muddy tidal altar
a watery enmeshed world as tide pulls
back revealing a *prasad* of crustaceans
a pulsing orchestration of life

Hover over these exposed muddy margins
slip into the skin of your animal and listen
mellow piping whistles rise
probe into the unknown places as

the bills of dunlin, sandpiper, whimbrel
through the gate of belonging return

The pull of moon on the sea is prayer
a circumscribed cycle of love and grief
reside in this entanglement
sit here, offer your attention

*prasad: a devotional offering made to a god, typically
consisting of food that is later shared among devotees.*

LITANY OF DAWN

From the shore a silent form
the shape of water
slips into the shadowed pond

the second then the third deer
received

the fourth leaves the shore
gliding through her dark waters
I understand this a kind of initiation

slow return of light
from the southern edge where
pond bends quiet gods cross

When that which separates dissolves
in the luminous wind   we awaken

poems are navigations

i would be lost without their making

long before our current age crystals of Icelandic spar

were used on sea voyages to navigate the course of a vessel

the hidden sun refracting a prism of light

OSEL LING | Pampaneira, Spain

Late morning sun dries my one bowl
Wooden pegs pinch a red-checked dish towel billowing in the wind
I observe how it curtains the mountains from east to west
Notebooks contain fragments, stones as fragments so whole
Bend of a wild apple tree its ripening fruit the size of a child's fist
A small pile of almond shells
A slab of oak, a wedge of grey schist
I sit on the shadowed wall of a stone *cortijo* the sun moves west
Voices of azure-winged Magpies received as coarse prayers
Persistent hum of cicadas carries this moment to the next
I take refuge in the arched chamber, a resounding bell
Chants from the unhurried slope of distant hills
Pages of a borrowed book move through
their thousand lives

Hold a pond to the light
you will see poems
even shrouded in fog
you see light
Sesachucha Pond
in dawn's low voice *Sack-a-juh*
here the eastern rim of the earth
conspires with the Atlantic
there is no place that
does not see the water
does not see you
suffused with brilliance
floating torso of a Striped Bass
leans into this light
in beauty we are made visible

AFTER STONEHOUSE (1272-1352)

I was a poet who didn't know poetry
until i moved to the mountain -
and learned to hear the speech of chestnut
the mellifluous rippling of poplar
I listened to the river its winter adagio,
spirited in spring
Birds migrate over the Straits of Gibraltar
mountains encoded in their song
First hours of day, the sky cloudless
wearing the land around me like skin

bone is loss bone is memory bone is the empty space within prayer bone is blue and ebbing bone is littoral bone is silence bone is the spiral of time bone is light captured and held bone is the traffic of waves bone is the weight of love

bone is exploitation violence ignorance bone is hearing bone is wisdom bone is mother bone is forgiveness bone is of the wind bone is cancellous and receiving bone is correspondence

bone is the song swimming in the moon

small birds tease daylight with song
pushing down to earth each strand of night

This morning I speak of the simplest
things   sky   river   the dry earth
settled on the wooden table

In the unborn future
with the knowledge of my mistakes
and the humility of forgiveness

I remap how i will live

Coyote's howl punctuates night fall
mind empties into hunger
the ferrous glow of mars
Those who forget the aliveness
of the world do not have eyes for darkness
Anchor not as trees
drift as shadows between
pine needles and ash
Fourteen billion years of radiance
compressed   have we forgotten
we harbor this earth
Sirius arcs south across the sky
intricately fretted sutures
guiding our passage

HENGE

We will go where earth
draws us down rooted like ancient oaks
where sky ties ribbons of worn silk
receiving stars whose radiance left long
before there were eyes to see
A ghost owl flies on silent wing
On the cusp of this fertile hour
Listen as memory weaves us back
into reverence from air and tats of down

Drawn by windsweep
Su suh su suh ray
Bending esparto grasses   coarse
Conspicuous hillsides of so many suns
To what god do we offer this worship
God of basket, of rope, canteens with pine resin
Something so humble celebrated
With this glorious reception of light

Into the bellied dark sun glazes
the ridge received as Angel's Peak
Morning light meets the mountain
Dawn in the valley incants
her language a sweeping wing
Sun struck and luminous
8 a.m. the arc of day begins
Light awakens the shaped and unshapen
Mountain breaths
Along the hillside goats graze
A confluence of bells permeates silence
Acequias coursing and elemental
Centuries of mingling water and stone
Water and stone   Earth remembers

A MORNING AT CLOVERFIELD

Because we are too busy
it will slip away fecund marshland
noble countenance of a Night Heron
it is here where the protest against loss
shifts beyond what is embodied

in between seasons as seas exhale
heaps and networks on tidal flats
of unnamed striving things
A love residency onto which
Sandpipers' bills jab

in the pause patience
draws down with the tide
sacred text etched by the feet
of rushing sand ploughmen
our minds move along the script
of spongy seaweed.

how to hold the broken sounds
of our surroundings
how to measure the dimming
of radiance

*during the spring migration in 2021 the number of Red Knots
counted on mid-Atlantic shores was estimated at 7,000
compared to 90,000 in the early 1980's*

FIRST OF MAY

A silver cloud of plovers moves
above a breaking wave
A helix of light rises out of a black hole
Scientists say it shouldn't affect
our corner of the universe

A deer rests among the reeds her head
tucked beneath her foreleg –
for a moment the world is embodied
in her stillness

I want to believe this violet pulse of energy
is the source of compassion, in each thing
finding its way back to wisdom

Weathered planks of wood, the flowering
beach-plum. Gentle recesses in the sand
await the pale-speckled eggs of shorebirds

DAWN | January light

The sky's longing for abalone
Organized by winter Sagg Pond speaks
glacial melt the weight of earth's impress
There is mystery in what has withdrawn
A place of correspondence
I toss a stone toward the center of the pond
Waiting for an answer
Singing back a stone echoes
Immanence anchors us here
Commits us to the aliveness in everything
The thrumming of hundreds of wings
lifts the inert stubble of White's field
From frozen to flow   low bass of earth
into exhilaration of air
Silence to thunderous *holy holy holy*
The heart records these ceaseless movements
breath, the tides, the restless earth

WHAT EARTH ASKS

Written with sand and bladderwrack
Sacred text of earth edged by coastline
Interlacing tidal creeks, marshland, oakwood
My boot taps the trunk of a fallen tree
giving its body back to earth
Membership into the world
Here I live deliberately in shared stories
wholly entangled lives and loss
Day forty-three of my father's passage
Through a lattice of branches
three hawks spiral
A sky labyrinth of flight
Wings bind grief with presence
Instructed to remain steady here
In this initiatory time my knees
press into earth

reading | tracing
an exquisitely layered world of tide-worn sands
migration's heave of wings across skies

seasons and cycles
refrains through the drift and spiral
Complex orchestration of nature's rhythms

taking refuge
in the shallows   seagrass covers rock
flash of silver wind birds   alight at the edge the tide

POEMS ARE FUGITIVE

Slipping through diamond-shaped
spaces   not easily tethered
not willingly tamed or broken
Poems are hemispheres of freedom
When we come close to them
even with innocent curiosity
they slip away disappearing
like the Great Northern Diver
beneath the waters surface
Stealing some of the light
leaving us with the unpolished sky
yearning to hold the world
differently

LET LIFE IN

mycorrhizae: a fungus which grows in association
with the roots of a plant in a symbiotic relationship

~

root to the land where you live

return to primary language attended by your eyes, ears,

the soft pads of your fingers

touch the soil, a depth of understanding awaits

an inclusive mind is informed by the senses

reach out to the plants, those in the forest, growing along verges

do not neglect the unseen kindom of entangled mycelial networks

be arrested by the fleeting mysterious nature of things

live in awe of the rhythm of earth's music, the screech owl's

tremolo, listen intently synchronized with your breath

see yourself in relationship with earth's wider wilder community

understand that everything connects everything else

even if you cannot take inventory of it

wherever you are honor what encourages life

receive through the soles of your feet

be humble (from humus "earth" hum of the earth)

learn to navigate beneath the stars

let yourself be governed by lunar cycles

shape new life with your hands daily

walk lightly

seek counsel from the trees, trust their wisdom

float in the sea, lose your ground

inhabit the slippery world of wrack and spongy stag seaweed

honor earth with sacred circles and ceremony

live embodied, love deeply
we are born into this beauty

In this fragile shelter of wisdom
may we remember our kinship
with the more than human world
may we be drawn into silent dialogue
with moss and algae, oracular roots
may we be instructed how to live
with equal parts awe and reverence
let ceremony arise within circles
of compass grass
orient us toward the expanse after
wave break as waters are gathered
back into the wilderness of the sea
let us shape anguish into something
sacred, something fierce and loving

ACKNOWLEDGEMENTS

Acknowledging the generosity of the kind folks who extended a place to shelter and write during the process of bringing this collection to life. Thank you, Tegan Campia, for your confidence and support.

To the land who never fails to remind me that I am held. Sierra Nevada, Spain, Sconset Nantucket, Cape Cod, Massachusetts, Outer Hebrides, Scotland, Faroe Islands, Sagaponack, NY

ABOUT THE AUTHOR

Walker, listener, intuitive | each morning a beginner.

Christine Morro writes poetry and creates art informed by the anima of the natural world, inspired by the sacred in the ordinary, the flight of shorebirds and the just after. Enlarged by encounters with the more than human world she seeks to enter this opening through a weaving back into our eco mythological story ~ to live the question 'how to belong to earth'.

Her writing is an offering to readers in the form of prayers, poems, incantations. A reminder to keep pace with the earth, to be entrusted to her longing and to navigate uncertainty with attention and presence.

Christine's poetry has appeared in *Reliquiae* published by Corbel Stone Press. Her prose and photography have appeared in *Minding Nature*, Autumn 2019 Center for Humans and Nature, *Landlines* published by Leeds University UK, The Pilgrim, Summer 2021, Flyway Journal 2022.

Christine Morro's Website:
christinemorro.weebly.com

ABOUT MIDDLE CREEK PUBLISHING

MIDDLE CREEK PUBLISHING believes that responding to the world through art & literature — and sharing that response — is a vital part of being an artist.

MIDDLE CREEK PUBLISHING is a company seeking to make the world a better place through both the means and ends of publishing. We are publishers of quality literature in any genre from authors and artists, both seasoned and as-yet undervalued, with a great interest in works which may be considered to be, illuminate or embody any aspect of contemplative Human Ecology, defined as the relationship between humans and their natural, social, and built environments.

MIDDLE CREEK's particular interest in Human Ecology, is meant to clarify an aspect of the quality in the works we will consider for publication, and is meant as a guide to those considering submitting work to us. Our interest is in publishing works illuminating the Human experience through words, story or other content that connects us to each other, our environment, our history and our potential deeply and more consciously.

Made in United States
North Haven, CT
11 December 2023

45576213R00067